THE MINDS OF OTHERS IS A DANGEROUS PLACE

Motto:

"Your first idea isn't always your best idea."

This book is unforgiving...

Copyright © 2021 by Darion Collett
All Rights Reserved
Designed by Darion Collett
Cover Photo taken by CHill Media
Cover Design by Adriana Rosales, Darion Collett
Edited by Bria Ortega
Printed in the United States of America

ISBN Number: 9798778700963
Library of Congress Control Number: 2021924693

Table of contents:
The Three Faces Of You……………....…..Pg. 13
Speech……………………....……..........Pg.15
Think For Yourself………………………....Pg.16
Be The Modern Mind…………….............Pg.17
Funny Isn't It………………………....…...Pg.18
Fortune……………………………..….....Pg.19
Midnight…………..…………….…...........Pg. 20
Part Of It……………………………....…...Pg.21
I Really Miss You……………….……......Pg.22
Welcome Back……………………….............Pg.23
Open Your Eyes……………….........Pg.24
Pulse………………………………….......Pg. 25
Who Do You Think……………….....Pg.26
Found…………………………..............Pg.28
The Grounds……………………....……..Pg.29
Go Back……………………………....Pg.30
Unspoken……………………..………...Pg.31
Run With Me…………………….…....Pg.32
Where Have You Been All My Life…....Pg.34
Host………………………………….....Pg.36

5

Voices……………………………………………Pg.37
Lets Flourish…………………………...Pg.38
Change……………………………………Pg.39
I Am Not Myself………………….Pg.40
Loop………………………………………Pg.41
Grew Up………………………………….Pg.42
Into The Light…………………………..Pg.43
Hey There……………………………Pg.44
Best………………………………………...Pg.45
Hm…………………………………………Pg.47
Personality……………………………Pg.48
Green Mind……………………………Pg.49
Don't Listen……………………………..Pg.50
Embrace You……………………………Pg.51
Endless Drives……………………….Pg.52
Finally……………………………….Pg.53
Reflect…………………………………….Pg.54
I'll Figure It Out………………….Pg.55
Its Ok Though…………………….Pg.57
Money Is War…………………….Pg.58
Twitch……………………………………...Pg.59
No………………………………………….Pg.61
Miscommunication……………………Pg.62
Another Time………………………Pg.63
Searched…………………………………Pg.65
Ha…………………………………………Pg.67
Wide Awake…………………………...Pg.68

6

Dance……………………………………………..Pg.69
What was it like………………………………Pg.70
Lets Chill…………………………………………Pg.71
You Left…………………………………………Pg.72
Friends For Now………………………….Pg.73
The Last Party………………………………………..Pg.75
Ignorance Is Bliss……………………………Pg.76
Ideas…………………………………………...Pg.77
Part Of Life……………………………...Pg.80
Whisper……………………………………….Pg.82
Becoming……………………………..Pg.83
Slaves Of Mind………………………..Pg.84
Are You Advanced…………………Pg.85
Inside……………………………………………..Pg.86
You Are You?.......................................Pg.87
Human Nature……………………………..Pg.88
Welcome To The Show…………………Pg.89
Coma……………………………………………..Pg.90
It's Possible………………………………………..Pg.91
From The Back Yard……………………Pg.92
Makes Me Think…………………………...Pg.93
Perplexed……………………………Pg.94
Time………………………………………………Pg.95
Love…………………………………………Pg.96
You Are My Sunshine…………...Pg.97
You Did……………………………………...Pg.98

7

Writer's Block…………………………………..…..Pg.99
Disembodied…………………………………..Pg.100
Brompton Cocktail…………………………Pg.101
Trust Yourself…………………………..Pg.102
Shoes……………………………...Pg.103
Stay Comfy……………………………Pg.104
Second Nature………………………….Pg.105
I Am Ghost……………………..Pg.106
Misplaced Dreams……………………….Pg.108
How To Get Back………………………….Pg.109
Hello……………………………….Pg.110
Fun Nights……………………………….Pg.111
Good Night………………………….Pg.112
Follow Your Heart…………………………...Pg.114
I Remember……………………….Pg.115
Found It…………………………….Pg.116
Cashing In Past Lives………………….Pg.118
Ourselves……………………………..…………..Pg.119
Least You Can Do…………………….Pg.120
Scam……………………………….......Pg.121
Angel……………………………………………Pg.122
Social Media………………………….Pg.123
Develop……………………………..Pg.124
Threads………………………………….Pg.125
Plot Twist…………………….Pg.126
Exist………………………………..Pg.127
Happiness…………………….Pg.128
Proven Wrong………………………...Pg.129
You Think I Don't……………….Pg.130

Fun In Dimensions......................Pg.131
Can't Come Back..................Pg.132
Stay True To You........................Pg.134
Madness............................Pg.135
All I Needed...........................Pg.136
Makes Me Happy.....................Pg.137
I Trust You...................Pg.138
Timeline........................Pg.139
Jealousy..........................Pg.140
Personal Eternity............Pg.141
Always Looking............Pg.142
Respect...........................Pg.143
Abandoned Profiles..............Pg.144
Become. Humanly. You.........Pg.146
Some I Live Twice.........Pg.147
Doing...............................Pg.148
Intuition........................Pg.149
Drama Rules........................Pg.150
Memory Blur........................Pg.152
Awkward.....................Pg.153
Time And Space..............Pg.154
The Alley.....................Pg.155
Illegal Skies..................Pg.156
Little Decision..........................Pg.157
True Words................Pg.158
Speak Up..........................Pg.159
Frayed..................Pg.160
No Hiding..................Pg.161
Your Shoes..................Pg.162
Accomplishments..................Pg.164

Sometime Later..............................Pg.165
Hatred....................Pg.166
Existence.........................Pg.168
Off Beat..........................Pg.169
The Note..Pg.170
Reply Please............................Pg.171
Artists......................................Pg.172
Guise............................Pg.173
Being Special..........................Pg.174
Sticks And Stones............Pg.175
Ancient............Pg.176
Betrayal......................Pg.177
Easter..............................Pg.178
Viewed...Pg.179
Acceptance..................Pg.180
How:How..Pg.181
I am Mine......................Pg.182
Inside and Out........................Pg.183
Embody...Pg.184
Sanity...Pg.185
Slightly Obsessed....................Pg.186
Healing The mind...............Pg.188
What I've Become..................Pg.189
Interesting Realization...........Pg.190
Mental-Mind-Special................Pg.191
Field Of Time....................Pg.192
Today............................Pg.193
Equal..Pg.194
Life Path......................Pg.195
Laugh a Little..................Pg.196

Times were Different.........Pg.197
Educate The Fool..............Pg.198
Talking To Yourself...............Pg.199
Change The World.........Pg.201
My Experiment...............Pg.202
Got It........................Pg.203
Our Own Way...............Pg.204
Different Paths..................Pg.205
Naive...............Pg.206
Lasting Forever....................Pg.207
People Remember Pieces Of You.......Pg.208
I Smell You...................Pg.210
Done With It..........................Pg.211
Don't Be Your Own Bully..............Pg.212
What's your name again?...............Pg.213
Matches..............................Pg.214
Dwell................................Pg.215
Kindness For Weakness............Pg.216
Staying...........................Pg.217
Smile.................Pg.218
You Don't Know What You Don't Know..Pg.219
You And Me...............Pg.220
What's Around You......Pg.221
THE WARNING......Pg.222
Want.....................Pg.225
Brain Malfunction..........Pg.226
Roll Over.................Pg.228
The Temple..............Pg.231
Say It..............Pg.236
Sometimes You Have To......Pg.237

In My Head Lives Static……...Pg.238
Things We Now Talk About……..Pg.240
Future Sight……………...Pg.241
The Day After……………Pg.244
A Few Years After………..Pg.245
Reincarnation……...Pg.247
Believe in You………..Pg.251
Righteous……………Pg. 252
Face………………..Pg.253
Weak…..…………………………Pg.254
Hero……………….....Pg.255
Overused…………………Pg.256
Eternal……………………..Pg.257
Hello Lovely………..Pg.258
You's…………………...Pg.259
Wonder……………….Pg.260

The Three Faces of You

Face number one exposes your shell to a world of distractions.
Facing the world
with smiles and valid interactions.
Joking about all of your personal distractions.
Be smart and intuitive.
Wear the face of socialization.
Face number one is who you are to the outside world.
The face you show to strangers.
Face number two is number one's best friend;
a companion in truth telling.
Radiating more than you want.
Loving.
This face holds your identity to those close to you.
This face is your reality.
Play your identity,
in a world of individual specimens.
All are living independently.
Face number three: restricted viewing,
straight from the true side of your originality.
A face that only you know. A face only you see completely.
This face is the real you,
in your world of secret visions.
Holding all truths unworthy.
This face is the true you.

Surviving solely in your mind's reality.
This is who you are.
Living in this world of vibrational synergy.
The true you resides where no one knows your true intentions.
Actual invisibility.
No one is who we think they are,
in this world of performing personalities.

SPEECH

It's not as simple as one might think it to be.
Powerful.
Sounds sink in so easily.
The words that come out...
They float on a conceptual possibility,
so fragile.
They control our existence in reality.
Once expelled,
they break the boundary of uncertainty.
Always invisible.
Expelled for eternity.
Never returning to the lips that let them go.
Those sounds slip out so easily.
An important substance.
One with no tangibility.
Once released,
they evaporate,
becoming a verbose symphony.

THINK FOR YOURSELF

No

    one

        can

            conclude

                the

            inception

                of

            your

        idealistic

progressions.

BE THE MODERN MIND

Living on this timeline.
Collecting bits of mind.
Imagination primed from the surrounding
modern times.
Prospects of our dreams,
stuttering from sight.
Stay in the right mind.
Intelligence is
airtight.
The greatest minds of time will
diminish.
Too bad their minds rot;
ideas go unfinished.
From the dictators of our
surrounding daily grind.
Time…
Time is not on our side…
Dwelling in imagination,
it's our own ideas we come to find.
Let your mind fight for distinction.
Be the modern mind.

Funny, Isn't It?

There are just some things
    you shouldn't take for granted.
The love projected was never nurtured.
Whispers and words,
    always ignored and directed.
You thrived within your boundaries
    from unforgiving hatred.
Never giving a chance to
    the one who deserved it.
I always showed up when
    your needs were deserted.
It was always my turn to
    come back feeling shattered.
Never did I take for granted
    what I knew was true.
You never loved me.
    You always loved
  you.

Fortune Teller

Miscommunication completes your realization of devastation.
Your words ring with truthful words of misfortune.

MIDNIGHT

Midnight rests on swollen dreams.

Waking up your incoherent schemes.

Rest assured by future sights.

This dream only lasts

for the current timeless night.

Wide awake with not a vestige of forward

thought,

sit back,

relax,

and let your mind rot.

Part of It

Why can't you stay
this age forever.
I want you to
stay little forever.
Growing up
can make minds
slump into
a torpor.
Stay curious about your
conscious endeavors.
I will always love
you the same.
Though, I know your
memories of me won't
get better.

I REALLY MISS YOU

"It's really disappointing to see someone you love not care that you're trying."
At that time and place,
it was my own heart that was dying.
I would do anything to go back.
Now I'm here secretly crying.
You were lost too.
I couldn't help!
I was stuck surviving!
The people I thought I loved left me brainwashed.
All their actions conniving.
You loved me for me.
And I always loved you for trying.

WELCOME BACK

Nothing leaves you like
the way you left yourself.
Did you leave
with thoughts of
self-help?
Dismal care of self-repair.
Just restore "you"
before you get back here!
You stood still,
stranded at that juncture.
You are you now.
That's
ALL
I've been
waiting for.

OPEN YOUR EYES

Slowly the light wakes me up.
It's another day that I must get up.
Heart racing uncontrollably.
                    I can't keep up...
               The fears that haunt,
                 they just show up.
Why must I be made this way?
Someone please suture my eyes shut.
I must get up...
I don't want new sunny rays.
          The sting in my eyes stays,
         the sting that life's proud of.
             "I have to wake up!"
         Through a veil I step out of,

                      and sit

up.

PULSE

                    Lights going down.
        In the crowd, silence passes.
Bewitching auroras of light
            entice us as the hush vocalizes.
Whispers and restless motivations mock
the entertainment of pulses.
My blood starts pulsing to the seductive vibrations.
          Tones easily stumbling off the majority,
      acting as its own entertainment.
             We,
    on our cloud nine thrones,
        lost in our harmony of movements.
         Eyes closed.
Feeling one with the vibrations and looseness.
     So penetrating it aches our bones,
       exactly where we all connect.
   The weighted air plunges deep into our lungs.
    Our minds run along chords and frets.
        Lost in the moment.
  Giving in to the pulses of musical geniuses.

WHO DO YOU THINK?
Worked to death by the Capital mind.
Living as slaves for all of time.
Forever existing in a world of fame.
First to work,
always to blame.
Fists of fury barreling down,
pushing our faces to the ground.
Built on selfish ideals, they smile;
we frown.
Just get past the money and frills.
Don't let temptation get you down.
They no longer feel,
practicing ideals,
they live as devils in beautiful crowns.
Why give the small people room to heal?
As if they don't think we can drown.
Enough is never enough,
no one seems to seamlessly fit into the crowd.
Profit, profit, profit.
Something we needlessly wrap our minds around.
Stealing our thrills, as addictive as pills.
Does anyone really care who sticks around?
Shut up with your incredulous trills.
You never planned on common ground.
In a world of kill or be killed,
you kill and disappear into the background.
Seems like you just want us to kneel,

back away, and bow down.
Making us look up to a disguised devil.
We idealize unsacred sounds.
You are our hope with no intention of rescue,
but we still follow while kissing the ground.
You're ill in the head.
Thinking you can control us forever simply astounds.

Found

Gaining confidence is scary. Once found, it changes your destiny.

The Grounds

Fly around the merry-go-round.
When you float up,
.
.
.
you must float down.
.
.
.
Static grins from plaster clowns.
Laughter radiates through the grounds.
Dewy grass in the midnight sun.
Wander around till you've
been out-spun.
Muggy air out-runs the fun.
A glow radiates on what's begun.
Disoriented minds.
Mischievous illusions.
Dreams come true,
on the rides with malfunctions.

Go Back

If only I could time travel back to our
old conversations.
Lies escaped so hastily through those rose
colored lips.
A trill of tasteless *vibrations*.
Oh the tails you'd tell about your secrets and
selfish motivations.
"She's strange."
Heavy words used for someone with too many
expectations.
You lie,
all the while I can see right through your
pathetic imagination.

UNSPOKEN

Belly up across the bed,

your voice suffocates my dread.

        Smile hanging off the side.

controlling Thoughts pushed

                      aside.

RUN WITH ME

I sit and ponder this anxiety.
Ahhhhh, my quiet house.
Yet...
These walls still smash me.
Weakness in my happiest of places.
A beautiful catastrophe.
Snarling,
your hands rip through my colorful spaces.
Colors I care to see.
Shreds of light,
I just see traces.
Fighting myself daily to become free.
Emerging with angst from my most shadowed places,
a battle that can't be seen.
This polluted headspace blinded my vision,
a place that needs no company.
Sometimes it takes awhile to find motivation,
to find the real meaning of
"me".

Hate yourself if you don't.
So I did.
So I won't.

WHERE HAVE YOU BEEN ALL MY LIFE

You ran through my life
without looking back.
You missed the marathon.
There's no
turning back.
There's nothing to chase,
I haven't looked back...
What's done is done,
you didn't come back.
I ran the race you missed,
and won.
Victory's sweet,
for the last one chosen.

There will be a next time to say something...
Won't there?

HOST

A virus cannot live without the host.
                    Regressing your
                            inner.
        It eats self-doubt.
    Embrace the virus as its host.
   This virus brings happiness to most.
The doubt it ate may bring unanticipated
               joy.
       Eating lessons, you didn't intend
to destroy.
          Let this virus live with caution.
   The easy way out isn't always
         the best
         option.

Voices
That laugh.
Sublime.
Plunging back
through concepts of time.
Thinking I could
never lose
you.
Those clock-ticks
never contribute.
Memories became
confined hardening statues.
Forever loving what used to be my truth.
Slowly forgetting
your consistent
happy attributes.
Lunging through time;
grabbing and
reaching for you.
That laugh gets distorted,
as time keeps on slipping through.
Time is healing,
as your voice
recedes from view.
That sublime voice…
Never saying words that are new.
I miss you.

<u>Let's Flourish</u>
Obsession with
the
future can
lead to
di*st*orti*O*n.
Thoughts connecting
will lead
to
fruition.

<u>Change</u>
Stay warm while the scene coaxes. Change isn't a hoax like you think it is.

I AM NOT MYSELF
The part of myself that I am not,
is myself.
I don't know who I am or who I will become.
Not every moment I intake I have chosen.
I have no specific path,
sometimes I feel frozen.
I'm getting to know who I am,
I've grown to live within reason.
Not knowing where personalities form,
I ponder on the subject of reinvention.
I'm now realizing who I've become,
someone who enjoys breathing.
Everyone else seems to know what's expected,
I ignore the criticism that's demeaning.
Validation used to be important.
Now I'm working on being comfortable with being.
I've learned to be me now,
something unexpected in this world of beings.
I am not myself.
Someone who is comfortable with becoming
reborn.
Surrounded by self-healing.

LOOP

You get caught on one idea that

    loops,

                   and loops,

and loops

    around
    in your world of
    morphed phobias.
    We are all living.
    Forbidden to
      hide from our
        own sense of

        hysteria.

Grew Up

If you don't love me
for me...
Then who do you love?
Do you love the shell that you
molded before
I grew up?

Into the Light

Bitter taste inside the light.

Light conquers

darkness,

    leaving no shadows in sight.

Deep coma of paralyzed blissful
fights.

  Demanding to listen to my internal burning

        light.

HEY THERE

Giddy and misguided is what
your mind revolves around.
Eternally stuck in your own head.
Effortlessly bowing to a **suffocating** sound.
Your standards
don't resemble a real person.
There was never common ground.
Living peacefully inside your blissful delusions.
You never wanted to decide.
You never made a sound...

BEST

Doing everything you can to be great.
Slipping up,
creates a bad taste.
People will never hesitate
to put you down.
To get people to smile,
you need to frown.
When your victory is won,
you didn't win.
Someone is always better;
life slowly sinks in.
Why can't I be the best or come close?
Be the best you can be.
if you don't, you'll just coast.
Give up at becoming the best.
Become great
at what you love most.

Doesn't money drive you?
No.
Love.
I am driven by love.

Hm
Exceptional
  ideas radiate through the
  brain.
Consistent conclusions...
  Why can't yours
sustain logical calculations?

PERSONALITY

People will be
who they want to be.
A process of an ever-evolving
personality.
Never on the same page,
we often say
what we don't mean.
What lies in the eye
of the beholder
is a vision different in
everyone's scheme.
You are you.
And I am me.
Forever evolving our
personalities.

GREEN MIND
Your mind is green.
   It must be to stay where you know.
Those that take,
   will reap what they sow.
Kneading our minds.
   Worshiping innuendos.
Your green mind then slips
   to believe what's been sown.
Live in the green mind,
   it's the pristine knowledge to know.
   Only green minds will reign supreme.
Mind control practiced all on your own.
   Take control,
before your mind is caught scheming in
someone else's role.
   When you know the truth
your mind will be freed.
A new kind of glow.
   Cut out the subconscious of mankind.
Mankind's mind develops quite slow.
Love yourself.
Develop a green mind.
Free your soul.

DON'T LISTEN

Don't listen to what others say.

Jealousy shouldn't win this conversation.

I will love you 'til the day I die.

Never with conditions.

Without you,

I'd lose all of my motivation.

Together we create

an unstoppable

determination.

EMBRACE YOU

Learning,
growing,
aging,
changing.
This life
is yours
to live.
Embrace who you are.
There's no need for changing.
Be you for you.
Make life worth living.

ENDLESS DRIVES

Searching on this journey.
Mountains beam serene.
Looking blurs my vision.
All I see is green.
Miles and miles between my homes.
The miles with you were always fun.
Long hours pass
driving through green.
I never ever want to leave this scene.
The trees pass by so fast.
Driving with you was simply the best.
We would talk the whole time,
none wasted on rest.
Without you now,
it's boring.
The foliage wilts, depressed.
Even the music isn't the same.
It has magically digressed.
Everything blends into this long, green, blurry
stretch.
A scene only as beautiful
as the current timeline forecast.
Sublime times are where your smile rests.
Rest in Peace.
Remembered by this long, green, blurry, stretch.

Finally

When being yourself gets others to where they

don't want to be.

You,

my friend,

have been

set

free.

Reflect
Open your mind.
May these words ring
sublime.
Your mind will sometimes rot,
corrupting what's pristine.
Refresh your thoughts.
Listen to your dreams.
Scheming with intellect
of reflective thinking.

Of reflective thinking,
Scheming with intellect.
Listen to your dreams.
Refresh your thoughts,
corrupting what's pristine.
Your mind will sometimes rot.
Sublime.
May these words ring.
Open your mind.
Reflect

I'LL FIGURE IT OUT

Glowing in your bubble,
    you walk with a smile.
God knows you've been in hell for awhile.
    I love you with all of my heart.
These words...
Like a vow,
    till death do us   part.
Your words are exhaled like laughing gas fumes.
Radiant with love,
    that gift consumes.
Always focused on everyone else,
    helping them crawl from
their personal hells.
Lingering inside,
the cracks of distress strengthened.
    The world started to
wring you dry...
A hollow heart giving out good *vibrations.*
But right now,
    this good heart feels lost and
forgotten.
The truth could not be denied.

The choke hold tightened.
Then for a moment the world brightened!
This soul had almost lost its desire to thrive.
    Simply trying to be outspoken.
Her bright light is taken.
Crushed before the win,
    continuing on to live in realms unproven.

<u>It's Ok Though</u>
Practice who you want to be.
Living life means conforming to uncertainty.

MONEY IS WAR
Who has money to waste anymore?
You're expendable in this monetary war.
"Money is not happiness."
A fact they've made up.
Our happiness is determined by the investment trust.
The wealthy tell us that money is lust...
All the while we survive just to be broken.
A gift to us?
"Money is not happiness."
A lie thrown at us.
Money is happiness in this world.
What an interesting development in human selfishness.
In a world,
where
money equals
bliss.

TWITCH

Sit.

Listen.

Fingers twitch
with silent hesitation.
      The exhale sings with verbal frustration.
There exists limits to expectations.
         Uninterrupted thoughts argue and race
with impatient solutions.
The ringing between my ears connects me to the next
set of oncoming emotions.
Lighting stings my veins, triggered by mind numbing
provocations.
Straight down to my feet,
my toes twitch with residual tingling sensations.
Eyes roll back as the blackout exceeds my expectations.
I need a break.
A break from thoughts and past decisions.
  A novelty idea with this sleep deprivation.
     I often question these minds we own as a human
             creation.
The body.
A connected system where

thoughts create physical reaction.
Peace will come in due time.
There is peace in self connection.

No.
  Detangling the
    metaphorical concepts of life.
  Your mellowing memories give peace to my
wandering mind.
I miss your support of even the simplest things.
Your laugh lives quietly in my memory where
your tone-deaf self sings.
  Please cuddle me in your arms forever,
a place I'll never stop missing.
Every night I look up at the moon
and catch myself
      reminiscing.
I will always think about you.
Your smile I'll see when
    I'm dreaming.

Miscommunication
Miscommunication
completes
your realization of
devastation
with truthful
words of
misfortune.

ANOTHER TIME
You wish for me to forget who I am.
You run with this thought.
Now go!
Run as fast as you can!
This dream I didn't get then,
but now I understand.
You know,
I used to wish we were friends.
Confounded by the lies,
trapped from beginning to end.
I do promise there was a time,
when I thought
your thoughts could mend.
I thought I could love you.
Then those dreams became banned.
One day,
I don't know what we will realize,
but maybe we'll pretend.
Pretend you didn't exist
in my life, or that you forced a plan.
'Til then, I know you will despise
exactly where I've been.
You let me believe your lies.
Empty truths were always given.
I would've loved to believe your lies,
if I wasn't my own person.
The way I am made is different.
I live within my reasons.
Your world is broken.

I need to shine with my own skepticisms.
I cannot change who I was.
Who I was still answers to who I am.
Your insight is flawed,
I need to master my own plan and life
visualization.
Making you listen
takes more effort than I prefer.
There was a time when I wanted to love you,
but it all felt so forced.
I may have loved you once,
when the terms weren't yours.

Searched

Finding issues

where there were
  none.
I'm sorry for the
    issues
       complicatedly

          spun.

HA

Accomplishing goals I
planned
when I was young.
Accomplishing
goals only
I have done.
You will take
credit
for me, I can
already
see.
I know your
guilt
resonates with
my life
deposit
capability.

Wide Awake

Wake up and breathe.

Inadvertently needing to be healed.

Hungry,

our souls eat virtual thrills.

Distrust in our own bodies.

What we crave deceives our own

skills.

From the moment we wake...

Do you check your phone first

or meditate away the world?

Wide awake like a nonstop nerd.

Self-care.

Often overruled by the

nonstop social world.

Dance

        When at home,
                            dance,
with all of
           your own
intentions.
        A moment
                    of peace
        gifts your
delusion.

WHAT WAS IT LIKE?

Crazy fun, those summer suns.

The night is young. Go have some fun. Run along with the waning moon. Magical dancing while visions ensue. Back in time, when the world was new. Dancing with the distant sun. Remembering silently how the moon would swoon.

LET'S CHILL

In this social setting of people you don't know.
Just for that moment.
Everyone puts on a show,
a front,
to be who they're not.
Music and talking,
it's all a blur.
Eyes giving up.
Mind spinning.
Disturbed.
I just keep
hearing
words.
Dance to feel the moves.
Keep going;
don't lose your groove.
You have nothing to prove.
The music becomes your mood.
Drift around;
don't lose your nerve.
Does this moment feel like happiness?
Composure disturbed.

You Left

Looking into your eyes
I quietly gasp.
Please never leave my grasp.
You don't hear it, but I do.
The quiet whispers,
and the silent
'I love you's.

FRIENDS FOR NOW

Silky smoke envelopes the air.
It's cold as hell.
The night is still.
Where would you rather be
than here?
Conversations emit emotional chills.
These people are your friends.
Don't choose regret when enjoying a current
thrill.
This setting is fun in retrospect;
time stands effortlessly still.
Friends come and go as they please.
Camaraderie,
a practice older than the developed world.
Friends come and go.
Enjoy the time you have.

Rest is a freedom.
Easily addicted...

The Last Party
This scene isn't all I expected it to be.
Living is quite surreal in all actuality.
Surrounded by people that I love willingly.
This beautiful life I live truthfully.
I love them all...
Almost completely.
Most of them dazed,
seeming otherworldly.
At the end we leave this place,
technically early.
We were all here once.
Now we all won't show up again
accidentally.
It's the last time we will be together.
We leave.
Nonchalant and happy.

IGNORANCE IS BLISS

IGNORANCE IS BLISS

IGNORANCE IS BLISS

It's amazing how stubborn people can be.

Small ambitions create personalities.

Move along with your little catastrophe.

Catty moves you're making,

but I'm not scared, you see.

Ignorance is bliss,

blinded by humanity.

Ideas

Don't let dark ideas surround your success with nonchalant conclusions.

I am always...

And some people think they have **anxieties**.

Ha!

The ones who know are allowed to **laugh**.

Part of Life

I played while you ignored me.

A part of my life I'm surprised you didn't see.

Turns out you will never know me.

Leaving the life you suppressed

is how I became *the best me.*

"I don't understand how everyone sees you as this amazing person."
Just look a little deeper.
Maybe you'll find a reason...
Those words broke my heart.
And you didn't even hesitate saying them.

__Whisper__
I am not going
  to whisper
 soft promises.
  I will raise
 my voice
  or it'll lose
   its progresses.

Becoming

*Find endless determination.
Release the hesitation
behind all of your contemplations.
Don't postpone.
Become what
you're
given.*

SLAVES OF MIND

Made-up place,
in a made-up world.
People think like you, don't they?
Word for word.
You think you know it all.
Living in your own bliss.
This enslaved mind you own,
is very hit or miss.
Everyone's mind is different,
you know this to be true.
You ignore this bliss,
hoping that it's not just you.
The minds of others is a dangerous place.
Too much upkeep at this fast pace.
Think like you;
others do not.
Think too hard and your mind will rot.
Continue your bliss,
in this made-up world.
Confide in yourself.
Ignore what you've heard.

Are You Advanced?
Don't waste time;
it all goes fast.
Humans consistently waste time.
Retaining opinions that
shouldn't last.
Concepts driven by your mind are your push.
Continue growing
in your made-up world that's
rushed.
The conceptual world is controlled by your own
hands.
It's up to you.
Create how you advance.

Inside

I don't care what I look like,
and neither should you.
Concentrate on what's inside to be true.
The inner-self resides on high.
Living in your head,
reflecting on different times.
Ideas alone should self-identify.
Believe in yourself.
Find endurance
in your head filled with
charismatic cries.

You Are You?

We never are the way we pretend to be.

In your head lives the real you.

                                              Sitting in

uncertainty...

Human Nature?

Deceitfulness rules over the nature of human bliss.
It's a generational greedy business.
All the way from pharaoh to princess.
Those that rule
get there with deceit.
All very capable of making choices.
The feelings that rule bring defeat,
covering all small voices.
Human nature is bliss
while maintaining
deceitful
choices.

Welcome to the Show

I became
your newest
creation.
Somehow proving your
selfish
motivations.
I was the show
in your circus of
expectations.
A living being
that you controlled
when it wasn't
your decision.

Coma

You will linger in my mind forever.
As time goes on,
my mind runs hot
like a rampant fever.
Constantly thinking of how to change.
All that I accomplish is a thought
inducing *coma*.
I'm now starting to surround myself with
people who
believe in *karma*.

IT'S POSSIBLE
Life so fragile.
Thoughts so serene.
How was something made so pristine?
Never in darkness.
Forever emitting a gleam.
Always bringing happiness
and bliss to the scene.
Sometimes I wish I could be you,
but I can only *dream*.

From the Back Yard

Cold, dewy air sneaks through the window.

A feeling magically surreal.

Waking up giddy,
to this beautiful, refreshing smell.

Breezy caress of the air tickles my cheeks with its floral melodic skills.

Deep freezing breaths,
leaving behind a trill of chills.

Slowly I slither back under into
this thick blanket-layered shield.

Becoming distant from today has awakened a harbored thrill.

These sublime moments.

Hidden beneath the sheets
in a magical cotton world.

Makes Me Think

Considering where I
should have
    been.
Sheltering my views
on where I
could've
    been.
I still wonder
what gave you
    motivation.

Perplexed

Browsing past where thoughts

steep in plain

sight.

Rolling backwards into plans fought for

with spite.

Growing a presence takes tedious

connections.

Simple ideas remain stuck in the

human mind of

perplexing

temptations.

Time

There are so

many ways that

you can look

at

time.

What was yours for an hour...

lasted an eternity in mine.

Love
Love.
What an interesting word.
Meaning so much and so little,
this word always occurs.
Some give all,
and some give none.
This word means the world if correctly spoken.
Love is full of misunderstandings unwilfully done.
You'd better mean it,
when you say that
you love someone.

You Are My Sunshine

The sun on these days never turns grey.
Here in my heart,
                              with you gone,
is your new place to stay.
                              As the sun
beams down
                              it surrounds my warm face.
It's almost like I can touch the lipstick you left on
my cheeks.
The sunshine remembers what life used to be.
You are my sunshine.
A song for you and me.

You Did

You made my life a competition.
Using me to create distance
from those who spit comparison.
What win are you waiting for
in this mind-bending competition.
There's still critiques not factored
into these scenarios of criticism.
I'm still me,
sometimes controlled
by potent comparisons.

Writer's Block

Writers

block

I know it

well.

In fact,

it's happening

right

now!

I have no

subject,

just a brain

teasing disconnect.

No letters to

write my words.

Their meanings, I'm

struggling to

project.

DISEMBODIED

To say people don't
change is a form
of manipulation.

I bet you've changed
one opinion in this
continued conversation.
Thinking doesn't take a
whole generation.
Manipulate thoughts
for your own
satisfaction.

Your mind being
the ruler overall.
Consciously creating your own

disembodied
sanction.

Brompton Cocktail

Subdued by the promises made up so clearly.
Chills engulfed the body with a cold surrender.
Shaking off the relentless, pestering whispers.
The body stays steadily aching under the pressure.
Slowly
slipping
unconsciously
further.
Eyes
now
open
to
a
newfound
contender.

Trust Yourself

I've noticed a pattern as of lately.
The outside perspective succumbs
to visuals of controllability.
Forbidden to speak what I feel,
I smile,
bright as a daisy.
Contorted thoughts visit.
Rapidly breaking my vision of reality.
Living in a puzzle can be quite troubling.
Stay true in a vicious world so unforgivingly
appealing.
Life is living in blissful uncertainty.
Sometimes the balance isn't so forgiving.
It absolutely matters how we get back up to
start smiling.
In the end,
the search for happiness
is finding the strength in living.
Take pride in becoming a trustworthy human
being.
Smile.
Take control
of your self-identified ability.

Shoes

Put yourself
in my shoes.
Even though, I will never put myself in yours.
It's your job to understand what "I" stand for.

Stay Comfy
Don't get comfortable in one way
or another.
Comfortability leaves room for growth
in a life of **stutters**.

SECOND NATURE

There's a lot of normalities that should have come second nature. Those ideas never consistently became an idea that was nurtured.

I AM GHOST

The lies you told yourself were truths you
never
thought would unfold.
I loved you.
I'm just not as bold.
I keep to myself,
hoping it's the truth you've told.
My restless ways make me
look selfish to most.
I am who I am.
I wish you'd love me
like how you've loved all your ghosts.
Suffocating,
my chest breaks
with what I know.
My soul is straining to
become what you love most.
I will continue to be me.
Your selfish,
hollow,
ghost.

I know it sucks for you that I still find ways to

smile.

Misplaced dreams
Running around in
misplaced dreams
The places I love don't exist on this plane
Butterflies fill my stomach
fluttering insane
Morphed up into multiple dimensions
astrologically stained
Going where existence will never need explained
The blurry lines of sin go unpunished
remaining unashamed
Continuous lies drift
controlling the ability to stay
Running into changing shifts in time
the walls change like a game
Questioning nothing
perplexed by my own face
My stay continues to be warm and welcoming
exactly where I'm misplaced
My misplaced dreams are where I am living
in this augmented reality I stay
Existence tricks me into believing
in a place where realities play

How to Get Back

Sit back
and relax
on this one and
only path.
There is no controlling others.
Fate will decide.
how you
get back.

<u>Hello</u>
Manipulation,
subservience,
and control.
These overused words slowly melt into
personal protocols.
Repeated terms in the realm of corrupt leaders
and life's riddles.
Become someone,
someone in a world with fewer master titles.
Listen to your destiny in a
world of mind-controlled idols.

<u>Fun Nights</u>
Stargazing
on this beautiful night.
I've never been more content than with
you by my side.
The horizon rests clear with no clouds in sight.
The dark outside surrounds us.
Glowing stars shine bright.
Laughing with each other,
trying to not be obnoxious to the sleepers inside.
You come back to my memories often
when
I think of happy
times.

Good Night

Reaching over,

you hold me still.

My body won't sleep.

My conscience feels ill.

You pull me in.

Sleep surrenders at will.

I'm tired of writing about you.

Follow Your Heart

*I followed my heart
like you told me
not to. I believed
my own words.
Deciding to stay
true.*

I Remember

Childhood drives
beneath cloudy skies.
The aura above me
turned grey with
a fight for whose
side?
Alone in the middle,
always overlooked.
Pay attention to what
matters,
not to what you're
hooked.
Your heroes should
not be competition.
Life is a crook.
Being part of you
wasn't my decision.
Ignoring life,
constantly reading
books.
Now I've lost both
over ignorant
decisions.
I don't want to look.
There should've been
love through all of the
contention.
Not a game-winning
smirk.
I found comfort in
solitude.
A win on my part.
Those skies above
painted my future.
And through it all
I never lost my heart.

Found it

Finding out who's
really there for you.
Others have shaped
what has become your
new values.
Mindsets change when
we grow and continue.
If they don't
love you for you,
then it's time
to discontinue.

Start being yourself.

Become who you want

to remember...

Cashing In Past Lives

Starting at the
beginning when
one just ended.
Welcome back to where
your celestial being resides,
thriving in a place of non-existence.
Jumping into the next too fast,
now my many lives are
permanently
inconsistent.
Elated to be here,
where dense beings reside on the plane of
persistence.
Here we
go again,
accepting our DNA disguise
of variations.
Cashing in the memories of past
lives,
living in daily dreams
that stay
coherent.

Ourselves

We constantly have
a craving for happiness.
Blissfulness,
not fearfulness.
        External maintenance
           exposes
        our internal wellness.
Constantly thinking
about why we are here.
Our personal game of
perpetual chess.
        No one will ever
       know the true meaning
         behind your
         blank stare.
    A tasteful look into endless
        thoughts.

Least You Can Do

Give others motivation when you have none.

___

When moping around in your darkest of times,

___

at least you could say you helped someone.

<u>Scam</u>
Idealizing
 what has become a
  mockery.
   As an
    intelligent
    collective,
     we need to achieve clarity.
Don't we have dreams to aspire to?
Dreams that change the scenery?
Use your dreams to shift the ways of humanity.

Angel

You are my angel.
These words still entice me.
The smell of you
I remember
distinctly.
Forever my love,
never love discreetly.
I thought I loved you then.
Now we're navigating our way
through eternity.

Social Media

The world fills our minds

with incessant expectations.

Perpetually looking and scrolling

through endless

choices of

brightly-colored solicitations.

Never even

giving a chance

to those with real emotion.

The day includes endless

scrolls through

life-altering

transitions.

An endless slew of interesting

motivations,

sucking you in with

knowledge and

empty reasoning.

Develop

I sit in wonder often. I have become courageous in this world of problems. Bending truths that have become less common. Developing myself in a world of criticism. Becoming me in a world of sexism. Underestimated, so I became a responsible creation. Myself, developing a mind that's capable in a world of mysticism.

Threads

Experience life for what it is.

Rip yourself from those dark mind-bending places.

Hang on to the ever-thriving thread of voices.

Swing,

the threads fly free from all dismal caresses.

Succulent words direct whose personality

possesses.

Swing back and forth

on those threads of chaotic messages.

These threads hold all knowledge to happiness.

Swing as directed.

Plot Twist

Even though the
    "I Love You's" stopped.
It might be easier
to let go than
  I thought.
No use getting

                                                      lost in
thought...

The disconnect is
     now the
  plot.

Exist

Existence sits
 on the
  inspirations of life.
What's created
 gives endless
advice.
  This art that's created,
we breathe,
 we live.
   This calling
 exhibits visions,
refined and unforgiven.

Happiness

Happiness is a
funny thing,
coming and going,
flying distances unseen.
It hits like hell.
Then it simply blows away.
Enjoy this moment.
It lasts for only a little while.
Reflect on true happiness endlessly.

Proven Wrong

Telling me I'll never be happy in any
relationship being the way
that I am.
All I can do is laugh.
I'm happier than you could ever
even imagine.
I can see jealousy envelopes
all of your decisions.

You Think I Don't
I'll never forget where
I was standing.
In the middle of that
bottom-floor-
apartment kitchen,
with the phone, in my
hand, ringing.
As soon as you
answered,
I started crying and
screaming.
You are forgetting to
love me.

You've changed,
all the while telling
me I'm exaggerating.
You chose for some
reason.
I still can't find an
answer.
To this day, I keep on
digging.

Fun in **Dimensions**

Sporadic dreams through visions
    behind closed eyes.
Reminiscing constantly on certain
    non-existent times.
Dimming so quick.
    Clinging on, I try to keep
    the moment alive.
Grasping onto visions
    from non-existent times.
Memories with friends
    I no longer know.
Their existence
    and my dreams collide.
Continuing on in the clouds, only
    seen by the mind's eye.
    Dimensions change while
        stagnant memories fight to stay alive.
    Dream on.
I'll continue to live where
    the dimensions exist to be mine.

Can't Come Back
Concentrating, I stare into your eyes.
They gleam full of happiness.
You use this as a disguise.
My whole world lights up with your enticing gaze.
I love you more than anything.
Please never go away.
You are special to me.
Your happiness wishes to stay.
Unreal bliss with you near me,
a magical entity who can't be erased.
I love your staticky hugs and kisses as they pelted my young face.
I took advantage of those mystical times.
Now I miss them with an angry disgrace.
You mustn't disappear yet and fade into space.
It's entirely too early for you to leave this place.
Please...
More memories need to be made.
Smile with me,
I don't want to wait an eternity to see your face.
We can never predict Father Time.
He has now taken your place.
I still see your smile
as it rests in my memory banks.
You weren't here for long,
but I really enjoyed your stay.
You were here for only a little while.
The good memories, always on replay.

I didn't make those decisions for you.
Your choice.
Your words.
My regret.
I should've punched you.

Stay True To You

Take advantage of all
   the small moments.
When your time is near,
    there's a chance of dissonance.
Live your individuality.
    Let there be no resistance.
Project love onto your loved ones,
   love with persistence.
You never know when it will be your time.
    Thrive through life with purpose.

Madness

   Madness.
A little exists
  inside of you and me.
Without it.
   We'd lose our humanity.
It is there,
   where we gain personality.
Conceptual madness
  created you,
 easily.

All I Needed

It's so sunny today.
Why don't you go out and play?
I'm going to relax for a while if that's ok.
I'll go out eventually.
This home is my sanctuary.
Sitting on my bed,
I watch my favorite show.
It's only on today actually.
No worries existed on these glorious, sunny days.
I'm with someone who truly loves me.
The love was never delayed.
You were all I needed,
bringing happiness even on your worst days.
Now I go back
and reminisce about those distant, sunny Sundays.

Makes Me Happy

I'm happy that, around me, you can be yourself. I want nothing more than for you to feel your importance. Know your worth. Be introspective. Be proud of every happy occurrence.

I Trust You
I know what I am doing.
Believe in me.
I know we've just met,
but, believe you can trust me.
Into my words, you listen carefully.
Left with no feeling.
That response excites me.
Be careful who you trust.
Everyone has a side you
don't see.

<u>Timeline</u>
*****Over time*****
*********your face will*****
return.
*********The true you*****
revealed
*****along these melodic*****
*****timeline*****
curves.

Jealousy

The people who hurt you the most probably don't even think about you. Even though, through **your** day to day, they are living vicariously through **you**. **Don't let them win.**
Let their insides fester with jealousy. Don't let their opinion overcome you. You can't change someone's opinion who doesn't even care enough to listen to you.

Personal Eternity

A breakthrough.
A want.
A personal eternity.
Do I wait longer?
I should've known
you'd give up internally.
How long can I wait for this so-called peace?
How much time is left of this journey?
I'll wait a little longer...
Hopefully I don't
give up completely.
Where were you when the ending needed
sweetening?

Always Looking

Never listening the way that you were
intended to by your yearning.
I have all of the answers.
But you still get *lost i*n endless *searching.*

Respect

You'll never know
how much
your smile meant...
You tried to lead
by example,
and for that
I'll always
have respect.

Abandoned Profiles

Scrolling and
  scrolling,
you'll never really know.
The comments left on that page,
    could've been posted forever ago.
That person you see,
    doesn't exist anymore on this plane.
Comments
  and tags abandoned;
reliving old trips down memory lane.
    Posts that were once a tedious endeavor now keep the loved ones sane.
      Souls living on as once-passing-thoughts,
forever existing in social
media's name.

*Why do I go back?
It's always a trap...
Always a trap...*

Become. Humanly. You.
You see a future that no one else sees.
Keep pushing forward.
Don't live to appease.
Appeasing the one and only person that is you.
Practice your talents.
Become.
Humanly.
You.

Some I Live Twice

Often journeying back in my mind through time.
    Memories that I love repeating stay in there,
thriving.
Those memories are all mine.
    I ponder on how magical it would be,
if for some,
I could live twice.
    Not all memories have a need for changing,
  some give back advice.
Some moments live on with euphoric thoughts,
 repeating only once in life.
    The power of memory bank motifs;
helping the good memories survive.

Doing.

Life is full of days doing things we don't want to do.
Pressing forward, performing current to-do's.
Persevering through moderate attempts at living.
Find a path to lean onto.
Create a path to strive for.
Sometimes the only way to get there is to do what we don't want to do.

Intuition

Pleeeeease don't fear your own intuition.

It is your special gift.

Never use it with discretion.

Drama Rules

I now understand why people thrive on drama.
    Why think for yourself?
What gives you the right to cause intentional trauma?
    The drama abroad from yourself
lives with no intentional commas.
    Relishing in this life they live with no consequence or persona.
When the drama isn't yours,
    your brain thrives
with reassuring
    karma.

Just give me some time. Just give me some time.
Just give me some time. Just give me some time.
Just give me some time. Just give me some time.
Just give me some time. Just give me some time.
Just give me some time. Just give me some time.
Just give me some time. Just give me some time.
Just give me some time. Just give me some time.
Just give me some time. Just give me some time.
Just give me some time. Just give me some time.
Just give me some time. Just give me some time.
Just give me some time. Just give me some time.
Just give me some time. Just give me some time.
Just give me some time. Just give me some time.
Just give me some time. Just give me some time.
Just give me some time. Just give me some time.
Just give me some time. Just give me some time.
Just give me some time. Just give me some time.
Just give me some time. Just give me some time.
Just give me some time. Just give me some time.
Just give me some time. Just give me some time.
Just give me some time. Just give me some time.
Just give me some time. Just give me some time.
Just give me some time. Just give me some time.
Just give me some time. Just give me some time.
Time wasted.
Goodbye.

Memory Blur

Memories blur in with my dreams.

I cannot seem to disassociate what is real from this existing timeless plain.
When am I me?

Am I me in these dreams and solid memories?

Appeasing these thoughts is a relentless job,
a pathological tease.
Put my reality back together...
Please?
Help me make sense of this dream land of realities.

My memories are exactly where I have lived with beings of ease ...

Reality is bliss when you live in your dreams.

Awkward
Awkward to be myself.
Skin on.
no control.
Be you.
Thinking you can't.
Stopped by nothing.

Time and Space

Time and space:
the glue of existence.
Do what you will.
Be who you are.
Heaven and Hell.
Those planes are human ideas.
Argue with God?
What's his response?
He has none.
The answer is within.
Be you.
Survive for your dreams.
Existence has its theories.
Don't give up on intellect.
Time and space,
both equal
you.

THE ALLEY

Running down the streets I know best.
This is my home.
Memories create this beautiful trance.
    On my way to the secret shortcut, I hustle.
I see it up ahead, lined with a vine-covered fence.
As the leaves and trees lean in,
I smell the fresh scent that they possess.
The wind whispers softly with
    a breeze that helps my mind rest.
Blue skies above me.
    They sure love stealing my breath.
Uneven,
    my feet trip over the asphalt.
All of the edges a mess.
    This is my favorite way to go,
wading through the magical vine tresses.
The sun stings my face as
    my hands graze along the
vine-covered fences.
At the end of my secret alleyway,
I take in a deep breath.
Closing the gate behind me,
    I keep walking down this
street I know best.
The alley. The place that absorbed
all of my childhood secrets.

ILLEGAL SKIES
Beautiful.
Your sparkling eyes
embellish your disguise.
I will always want to look at you
in this moment.
A moment dressed in
illegal
skies.

Little Decision

This time it's my turn to make the little decisions.

A modern time,

with modern comparisons.

Happy that

no one will ever get in the way again.

Leave me alone

with my well-deserved thought

relaxation.

True words

  I will always be waiting to appreciate the true words never
     spoken.
How, in those eyes, do I not look
    broken?
Those words that came out...
    They held no meaning when
     spoken.
Of course I feel nothing.
Your true words ring
     deceiving and open.

Speak Up

Shut up.
It's my turn to speak.
No more lessons on how to alter my mind please.
My inner dialogue deserves to think freely.
You don't know what's best for me in my world.
Are you having fun with your manipulation recipe?
Conversations of ours spin around and around in my head.
Repeating and repeating on rotation in my sleep. Beating you at your own game makes me feel anxious; and free. To you I will never win in your made-up world of strategic lying.
I'm happy in this new world of mine.
A place where I can no longer hear you talking.
Understand what I speak.
I know you won't listen when I open my mouth anyways.
I'll always speak up for myself.
You never stood up for my psyche.
You won't accept my freedom to choose.
I don't need your permission in my new world of awakening.

Frayed

A means to an end.
The end.
The end is the beginning of mending.
We Need Constant mending.
My Body now feels the give and bend.
Frayed.
Easier said than done.
We need a new beginning.

No Hiding
  Don't
become
your own
demise.
  Crying
  for help
   behind
other's eyes.
    The
  bitterness
will stand
out with
    time.
One day
the bitterness will
   control
what others
  look at,
when they
  see your
  smile
   shine.

My Shoes

Walk a million
in mine and
I'll walk a
million in
yours.
Knowing
what you
love is how I
remember.
Loving who I am,
and who I will become.
Walk a million in my shoes.
understand the unknown.

I'M SORRY I TOLD YOU NOT TO SING.

I'M SORRY I TOLD YOU NOT TO SING.

__Accomplishments__
Why does doing
    what we love
terrify us? Why are we afraid of
    judgement?
Isn't making yourself
    happy
enough of an
    accomplishment?

Sometime Later

Your face is beautiful and
   resentful.
I love you so much.
I know you don't feel
   the same though.
When we talk the conversation
   always has potential.
I might say a
   few dumb things,
hoping that, on the other end,
   there rests a smile.
You've grown up.
I've now lost hold of all my
   emotional signals.
I'll always love you.
Don't waste time on me
when growth for you
   means I need to be
discontinued.

Hatred

Hatred.
An interesting motivational tool.
The bitterness of the soul
makes our fragile life intangible.
Our souls live on.
Rigorously learning from what they have been shown.
Our immortal souls need the flow of yin and yang,
so we can learn and grow.
Hatred is easy.
Healing is slow.
Hate forever,
and your soul will never grow.

I miss you with all of my heart.

I just hope you still love me in yours...

EXISTENCE

We're choking,
climbing up this beast.
No gloating,
just floating in what the mind sees.
Looking like fleas,
what a nuisance to please.
Full of greed.
A contributing disease.
No need to please,
the hand waves to agree.
Aching,
our eyes start to freeze.
Crystallizing our lungs with modern debris.
Calm and still.
Eyes blinking with amenity.
Look into my eyes.
They blink empty, with serenity.
Coping minds thinking of clarity without becoming clean.
Lives scarily full of the unsightly.
Congregate here and roam the scenery.
All at once,
we feel the need to live freely.
These links of time
will bring together humanity.
Realize the hate
to avoid becoming a calamity.
Minds for now remain stuck in bodies.
We must survive together
as an independent family.

Off Beat

Singing
    off-beat.
        We don't
          stand.
          We sit
          on our
            feet.
          Sounds
          off and
          on. Belting
      out the lyrics all wrong.
    We'll never stop singing
all of these old songs. The
room gets quiet. Then we sing
again! Reliving our musical
past is beautiful when gifted
      with good friends.

The Note

You found the note that I stuck into hiding.

  Blank stare at the floor;

    and you just keep on yelling,

      using your power wisely,

        making me feel guilty for feeling.

    It was a long time again

      before I could write about my well-

              being. A healing process that I

          almost couldn't fathom beginning.

Reply Please

The talking subsides
and it's my turn to speak.
Nothing comes out;
        mind running rampant on repeat.
          Eyes darting back and forth
      patrolling my inner defeat.
           Never thinking that maybe,
              just maybe,
I don't care to speak.
Replying never helped;
everything you said left me on my knees.
              Why beg,
        when even the pain won't appease?
         I'll just keep my thoughts to myself.
              Mind in the trees.
      Silence,
    because my words would never please.
I stopped trying to impress you
      when being myself spread the disease.

Artists

As artists,
we love
what we do.
Never satisfied;
always continuing
to
continue.
A passion that stems
from unknown
familiar attributes.
Continuously creating
a vision with
no end,
an inexhaustible
point-of-
view.
A love that's only
gifted to few.
Only an artist truly understands
their personal point-of-view.
Through our eyes, we now
gift it to you.

Guise
We get to choose
who we let into our lives.
Choose wisely;
don't fall for a deceptive guise.
Personalities coat bodies with the consistency of
the wise.
I thought I knew who was behind your charming
disguise.
I've grown to choose wisely.
Seeing beyond your stylish eyes.
Through you and your endless you's,
are you kind?
Now being able to read the book you call your
mind.
Destroying the facts
because I studied your time.
I know what I've seen.
I'm finally listening to my own advice.
The truth will always lurk there.
Living through the soul behind your eyes.
You.
The devil.
Charmed up.
Living in an alluring disguise.

Being Special

My head wants to be in places it doesn't belong.
Why would you ever want to change someone?
It's important to know how to not hold on.
Being yourself should be special.
Everyone is someone.

Sticks and Stones

Sticks and stones are
          breaking bones,
but words need longer healing.
    Repetitive ties,
to a smaller world,
of "smarter" people singing.
        How much is really being learned
           in a time consumed by
                nonchalant forgiving?
        Steadily sculpting the minds
            of the young;
        effortlessly embedding
           untrue teachings.

Ancient

You're funny you know,
I will forever enjoy your company.
You smile and laugh at your own jokes,
personal hilarity.
I always appreciate your words of hope.
You speak while smiling with sincerity.
I know you won't be here for long,
so, for now, I enjoy your words entirely.

Betrayal
Funny, isn't it?
 A collection of words
 molded with misfits.
 Right from the beginning,
 your thinking was misguided.
 How were those thoughts of yours never corrected?
 Everything was blindly received.
 Intentionally directed.
 I can't fathom having respect for someone whose personality is completely fabricated.
 Now needing my own terms visually redirected.
 Realizing now how your thoughts were oddly initiated.
 Giving up on me was something that you must've intended.
 I gave up on you too,
 and I will forever mean it.
 Betrayal reigned
 like a polluted life sentence.
 Now I've learned to detect the meanings of words with attachments.
You're no longer the ruler over my being of limits.
 My pain got redirected into layers of progress.
 My ways of knowing
 are now truly ignited with lightness.
 A day and night comparison.
 I'll confess; I needed the lesson of pain to gain insight into deceitfulness.

Easter

One more! One more! Running,
my long hair whips me in the eyes.
Almost! Almost! I almost grab the prize.
Swiped, stolen, right from under my fingers
that are half your size. As you snatch
   that one, I run haphazardly to the next one.
   Giggling happily under this glazed cloudy
blue sky.

Viewed
People only know how to view
 from an outside
  perspective.
   Telling lies...

believing as a
 collective.

Acceptance

Perfection sits under-eye in the crease.
Don't falter.　　　　　Cross it out to
find inner peace.　　　　　No one
loved　　how your　　　　　love
was released.
　　They said they did,　　so the tension was freed.
Makeup running in your ears.
Listening made
judgment free.
Mascara trails stay
while laughing with us,
escaping from a
judging
passerby.

How:How
*How do you have the time?
I don't understand.*

*When you do what you love,
happiness won't have the time to end.*

I Am Mine

I can't wait to be
myself!
I've waited so long to
hear my own yelp.
Yelps of laughter
and crying all mine.
This journey has decided
that I am just fine.

Inside and Out

"It's all about the small things."
A phrase that takes
time to understand.
When you know someone
inside and out,
happiness can be planned.

Embody

    I have yet to figure out
who I really am.
  Embodying a soul I
    don't necessarily understand.
Awake and dense.
    Brain casually sitting in a regulated trance.
  I know who I am?
    I can't change
my own lens.
    Embodying this soul
  is more
troublesome than
    planned.
Bodies are temporary in
   this world that we're in.
Take care of the souls
   embodied within.

Sanity

You *chose*
the drug
over me.
The pull too
strong to set
you *free*.
You don't deserve
my love.
It's *gifted* only.
I chose to be sane.
Leaving *you* stuck
with insanity.
I decided to leave,
longing for
my own
clarity.

___Slightly Obsessed___

Steadily obsessing over the spectrum of the unknown.
Death can't be avoided on this journey we are on.
I'm not the devil who indulges in chaos.
I live according to my own.
My thoughts stay where they fester, building what I personally condone.
Others judge my ways;
I enjoy living in these shadows.
I thrive in my molded darkness, happier than ever before.
For some, the darkness is light, when the people of light are wrong.
Where else would I go, when the darkness accepts everyone.
Obsessed with chaotic thoughts about what I will become.
I've become the best me in my darkness, created all on my own.

If we all love the same things,
then why are we so different?
What separates us?
Why create an unforgiving persistence?

Healing the mind.
Everything needs to be rationalized.
An upward prodigy-kind.
Leaving what you need behind.
Interested in new, progressive times.
Never repeating the old routine.
Going out in the world with adrenaline.
This new feeling... Eyes are open again.
Head in the stars, personal heaven.
Everything is a learning process towards healing.
Mind enlightened by my own well-being.
Interested in life; excited to be living.
Never going back to a mind that's unforgiving.
Diving in with a full mind, continuously rising.

What I've Become
I look back at my life with the great intent of learning.
Listing certain moments aloud,
I sometimes wish I could change things.
Breaking it down slowly,
like an estranged, psychotic being.
I was under the influence of a demonic human being.
I've grown since then.
The memories are pretty convincing.
Without all of my dark days,
there wouldn't be room for days full of sincere smiling.
I like who I've become,
but not totally in love with the journey.
I'm consistently trying
everyday to become a better person,
taking baby-steps eternally.
I'm becoming me in the body I
was gifted quite informally.
The idea of consciousness is a struggle
in my mind of misfit normalities.
I'm becoming me:
an individual
in a world of mockery.

Interesting Realization

I woke up one day
realizing that no one is who I thought them to be.
Unrealistic expectations changed my thinking promptly.
Find the truth.
Seek it internally.
Trust yourself.
Realize that only you know your truth completely.
Others will live their own truth whether you like it or not.
Live your life accordingly.

Mental-Mind-Special

Inside you grows the meaning of expanding potential.

    Everyone has a secret side.

The purpose of life occupies thoughts of misshapen upheaval.

Live in your own shapes.
Focus on yourself while others obsess over betrayal.

    Thrive while surviving in your very own mental-mind-special.

Field of Time

Walking together to a place all too familiar.
We come here all the time.
    Sky couldn't be clearer.
Sitting in the tall grass,
    our surroundings rest quieter.
We sit a few feet apart as we tie the long grass blades together.
    You look for clovers while I wear my creations of knotted grass-feathers.
    This grass is so long, long enough to hide my scraped knees from a successful summer.
    This old field of grass is a quiet safe haven from the world and its disorienting chatter.
    The air is warm,
it expands my dwindling patience with every specially picked clover.
    Thank you for being there.
I will forever-miss your presence as I walk through the grassy fields of time, dotted with sporadic flowers.
    The grass reminds me of you;
it sways in the silence of what I'll miss forever.

Today

I woke up this morning,
but today I felt different.
Today I didn't care about the unfolding
events.
I went throughout my day perfectly content.
Are there more days to come?
Well that's just life isn't it.

Equal

Why does it matter so much
where we come from?
All of the hands sculpted
are colored in
human form.

Life Path

Everyone lives on their
    own life path.
Why hate someone
    because they're different?
Everyone is different.
    A boring world would exist with the
same copy-and-paste people.
    I have never changed.
Yes I have.
Does anyone actually hear my voice of reason?
Is anyone really listening?
No one listens in this selfish world...
    Am I changing for the better?
Your "better" may mean discontinuing the people you once
loved.
Change is inevitable.
    Accept the differences.
Become yourself.
    Live your dream life.
Don't conform.
    Take control of you.
Why should everyone
    act the same?
They shouldn't.
They couldn't be you even if they wanted to.
    Be yourself in a
world that tells you that
    you shouldn't be yourself.
Be yourself in a place that thinks it can
tell you what to do.
Love your different soul in a world of judgement.
Your life path is driven by you and you alone.
Create your own world.
Don't lose yourself.
Smile through the judgement.

Laugh a Little

A small muse can really make your day.

Interesting to see the play-by-play.

The small things really do make life.

Laughing controls your smarter side.

Times Were Different

I never thought I would fully understand turning
your back on someone that you love.
You love me?
Even still,
I never gave up.
Love is never supposed to feel numb.
Love is supposed to build you up.
Love's light lifts you through all that goes wrong;
I got left reaching up.
Left behind, but strong.
I remember the cut.
I'm becoming who I want.
Thank you for giving up.

Educate the Fool

You don't know what you don't know.

Expand their minds.

Educate the fool.

Talking to Yourself

All things considered,
how could I not talk
to myself?
Am I the only one
here battling for answers from myself?
For the pull to be right,
I question my own questionable thoughts.
An ongoing communication
problem.
A personal plot.
Talking to myself
can't solve it all,
but it can solve a lot.
Daily, I have whole
conversations with myself.
Constantly working to solve these problems
with out-loud thoughts.
Demanding to be comfortable
in this soul-controlled robot.
I'm becoming who I'm supposed to be
when I argue with my own thoughts.

You are a disappointment.
NO.
NO.
NO.
NO.
NO.
NO.
NO.
NO.
NO.
NO.
NO.
NO.
NO.
NO.
NO.
NO.
NO.
Who told you this…?
YOU.
You are not a disappointment.

Change the World

The modern world is so confusing.
How long do we have to continue on with backwards thinking?
Suffering from rulers that have no brains in their heads lingering.
This world needs a break from stupidity.
At this point, we need endless forgiving.
This world is in dire need of an eternal change from what they've given our brains for feeding.
Killing our habitat while feeding on greed and useless winning.
Winning a game that we all play?
Eventually we will all end up dying.
This world has no future if we don't get enough energy focused on thriving.
Thriving as a species.
Working for the betterment of beginnings.
We mustn't continue on this way...
We don't want to end up as this galaxy's history of human beings.

My Experiment

You used me as an experiment.
  You thought I'd never learn.
   Forever balancing your views on the circumference of my differences.
  Often contributing a guilty conscience to my innocent mind of coincidence.
  Curious, I worked laboriously to figure out this unusual, projected, sick indulgence.
 Futures filled with happiness were broken with false promises of working repentance.
  I always knew where I stood.
  Your soul relentlessly lingered with annoyance about my existence.
  Turns out we used each other,
  up to the bitter end;
constantly keeping up a polished outward-appearance.
I'll always hold the truth close, just like you'll always stick to your story of lies and forgiveness.
An open-ended conclusion that continues on with our current state of existence.

Got It

You are the strongest person I know.
Smiling through the triggered pain.
Stay strong.
No sorrow.
I love you so much.
Don't let your head fill with disappointment.
Don't get lost and wallow.
Stay strong,
my love,
even if the pain always follows.

Our Own Way

We grew up far away from each other.
Far from where we originally started.
Getting separated from your soul ripped happiness directly out of my childhood.
Never knowing we
would meet again one day,
I searched forever with no information to get me started.
I kept up hope that we would reunite in this life.
A happiness I had missed dearly since we had been separated.
The universe knew all along about our connection, making us both wait for the perfect moment:
a reunion so sweet I still can't get over the overwhelming occasion.
I had found you, my treasure, the other half of my soul's best friendship.
Time *stuttered when* I thought you were gone.
I never gave up on finding you in this life despite opposing directions.
Then I found you!
Now we have more time together with no disconnections.
I will love you forever,
my one-and-only best friend.

Different Paths

People bounce around on different life paths.
Like a plan,
we all go the same way on these winding
freeway maps.
All of these different lives;
and you can only control your own.
All of these people engaging with others
on singular paths
unknown.
Be on the rise
in a world full of
frosted clones.
We all take different paths,
following infinite directions unknown.
The path you've chosen is different.
It's *all* your
very own.

Naive

Being naive in a lost world creates a blissful state.

Backup your conscience, don't get lost to a presiding maniacal fate.

Sit alone in this blissfully unaware space. Search your thoughts again and again for a static answer in space.

Religiously casting "lulls" in this game of hide-and-seek.

Lick your lips to the subconscious and its ideas about fighting flames.

Do you feel lost in this supposed comfortable place?
Push for answers in a daydreamer's glaze.

Think out loud with your intentions unfazed. Believing in delicious lies, are you?

Well, I blindly grazed...

Blissfully living unaware of the light being relieved from its rightful place.

Fictional truths from others dictated what I continued to believe.

Believe in the power of minds.
There are more ways to succeed.

Growing out of a naive mind will set your identity free.

Lasting Forever

Nothing really lasts forever.
Forever takes different stances on what we remember.
Forever and always.
What a sweet endeavor.
Sweet and succulent candies
grasp on, to dissolve and to add flavor.
The sweetness lives on through most constants and forevers.
Thinking that everything lasts forever
is a failure for adventure.
Nothing will ever last,
forever and ever...
Cocooned in current times
where the sweetness wins favors.
Linger in your sweet-filled thoughts about living forever.
Sit down and enjoy these candies
while the sweetness takes over.
Savor the sugar,
knowing that one day it will sweeten the memoir.
Be happy with your moments of sweetness.
Life is a short endeavor.
Never let go of the sweet moments.
Their flavor we will forever remember.

People Remember Pieces Of You
Remaining in someone's mind forever...
What a thought.
The memories they have of you...
you don't know,
but it's what *they* remember.
The good you-
the one you hope to live on in their minds forever.
The envious you-
the one that seems to linger in the minds of close-circle members.
The angry you-
the one that destroys favors.
The smart you-
the one that no one seems to remember .
All the "you's" make up your individual subconscious matter.
What others think shouldn't be what controls you   forever.
Their thoughts should never have had control over your mind or endeavors.
Who are you in others' thoughts?
You'll never know but it ceases to matter.
Stop thinking about what they think, or your mind will wander into the depths of

infinite answers.

<u>I Smell You</u>
Do not use my perfume.
We are not that close,
even in this room.
It's a personal thing to use my perfume.
I let you into my home.
A stranger's mind is misconstrued.

Done with It

I don't want to write
about depression anymore.
But I see you,
I see you
spiraling
and
spiraling
down some more.
I won't be there,
my help is
no more.
I see what's going on
behind those blackened,
sleepy eyes of yours.
I'm sorry it's your turn to feel,
but you must continue and endure.
It's not your time yet.
Get the story straight on
what you're fighting for.

Don't Be Your Own Bully

Be considerably careful about
how you talk to yourself.
Why incessantly hinder your
progress of self-help?
Self-help doesn't always come from
outside resources,
it comes from routinely learning about yourself.
Connect within to find
perspective.
Pursue the parts of you that hide and remain lost.
Connect the emotionally damaging thoughts
to what you've learned.
Listen closely to what your inner truth foretells.
Ignore the mind forever, and your body will feel like
hell.
The end of your time will project onto
what you've been building.
You've been building one hell of a tale.
Give support to your own creation.
Learn to expel.
Don't be your own bully.
Become an emotionally
freed infidel.

What's Your Name Again?
We don't know each
    other as
well as I'd
    hoped.
I'll simply slip you
back into the
    memory slot of laughter
where your smile
doesn't
    choke.

Matches

Our

souls...

Across the board,

they unmistakably match.

This fire is

lit with a match

unmatched.

--

!
!
!
!

Dwell

Why do you always
    dwell on the negative?
That's where I was
    put to thrive. You see,
it's my place of positive
    perspective.

Kindness for Weakness

Mistaking kindness for weakness is a common practice between people surviving in fear.
Sit; smile.
Move with gracefulness.
Expectancy reared its disfigured head, right up into my peaceful place of concepts.
Question all sounds from others mouths.
Their utterances will sink into your subconscious presets.
Solitude can inspire peacefulness.
Dictate and take control of your own wittiness.

Staying

Thank you for staying.
I'm so happy that you never
stopped believing.
Thank you for keeping me sane even
though we stopped talking.
Family is forever.
At least for the ones who never
stop believing.

Smile

Smile.
 Happiness.
  Bliss.
   Charismatic-slipped-grin
   on your call to dismiss.
  Smile.
   Happiness.
 Bliss.
Don't dismiss what can
 make someone's smile
 feel missed.

You Don't Know What You Don't Know

You don't know
what you
don't know.
Everything you
know is what
you know.
Judging you
on what *they*
don't know.
Give a chance
to let them know.
Only you will
know what you
don't know.
What you know
may not be enough.
You know?
Don't judge,
compare the unknown.
Think for yourself.
You know
what you
know.
Think again.
Learn the unknown.

You and Me
You
  and
   me
    we
     fit
      together.
     The 'I Love
    You' of
   tomorrow
links
us together
forever.

What's Around You

Pay attention to what's around you.
What do you do with that information?
Do you let it control your actions?
You only have "the now" to
make any and all decisions.
Time is wisdom.
Look at your surroundings.
Does your space bring you peaceful thoughts or is it chaotic from past tribulation?
Listen to your thoughts.
Are you in control of their direction?
Do you act on all of the thoughts that want to distort your current situation?
Do you let them misbehave and wander off in endless directions?
Can happiness be sustained in these biological meatbag creations?
Our thoughts…
We lose and gain ourselves back in every conversation.
Learn from past mistakes.
Our thoughts, in the now, create a future of wisdom.
Our thoughts: a creative world of individual ideas in a modern world ruled with manipulation.
Our thoughts.
We are free-form beings, stuck in bodies, living on a floating globe of water and vegetation.

THE END

Will you continue...

Ahead lies controversy…
Finish at your own risk.
The book ends here.
Will you finish?
Religion and "Me Too" reside here.
Challenges are brought to light,
and maybe more progress.
Close the book now,
if you're afraid of real problems.
I write about life,
a subject that we are all solving.
We are who we are
on our separate journeys of personal forgiveness.
Read on into my thoughts.
Continue,
if you dare to **finish.**

Did you say...

Want

At first, I didn't see the manipulation.
Like a poison that slowly disperses.
They kept a watchful eye through and through.
They easily brought me happiness,
all the while secretly focusing on the side of me
that haunts.
Did you mean those words that you said?
Or did you forget easily for convenience?
I ignored the most potent side of you.
I trusted you,
Until I recognized your true intent, your selfishness.
I mean, shit!
You laughed at my tears of disbelief and grinned at
my distress.
Your true colors.
A fucking narcissist.
I bet even the mirror lets you see what you want
when you cast your manipulative curses.

Brain Malfunction

Hearts race with confusion.
I see the pain.
The stain of love lingers...
It will always remain.
You cannot move on,
that I can see.
You call me crying.
"Just set me free!
I need to be
free!"
You beg and you plead.
Why can't you just see
what I see!
If you could see what I see you would
be set free.
I beg you to believe what I whisper.
You tell me I'm lying...
I don't know why I still beg you to
believe me.
With corruption in your ears,
nothing computes in your brain that's so
religiously fed.

Reality surpasses the lies that you anxiously use.
Reality is completely different between my head and your head.
You've jumped,
with no parachute
into a fire of "he said, she said"..
I refuse to think for you in the one life I've been gifted.
I will make my own choices, whether or not you approve of them.
I can see the sting in your eyes from what you perceive as "falling away from".
I am happy now with where I exist in these spiritual formulations.
I am happy this way.
Your head is filled with misinformation.
I wish you could see the good in where I have chosen to thrive.
I won't be changing who I am to fit the mold you've made for my existence.

ROLL OVER

Rolling over again?
For the millionth time tonight my heart beats in a rhythmic stinging.
Restless.
Restless nights aren't new.
Every night is a new chaotic beginning.
The body resonates with what the mind expresses.
My body;
organized with systems of lightning intertwined into my bloodstream.
These feelings...
Nonchalantly not sleeping has become my new specialty.
My mind races with infinite information.
Ideas linger, repeating and repeating...
Nights with these subconscious manipulations become a game in the dark.
Fan quietly spinning.
What is reality?
My vision stings with confusion from all of this thinking.
Caught in an empty headspace.
Roaming and roaming.
Rolling over for the millionth time.
I long for comfort

from another dimension of complicated existence.
This time should work according to my unreliable nightly calculations of sweating. Another night of hypothesizing the different meanings for life and realizing it has no ending.

"I've tried to kill myself a few times, but I must still be here because you need me to love you."

*Words that stung,
     but I understood...*

I love you forever.

You didn't deserve all of that.

THE TEMPLE
I love to see the temple.
I'm going there someday.
To fix the problems I don't have.
To listen,
stay,
and pray.
Hello to those suffocated by religion.
Listen to the direction of your heart.
Your questioning is needed for human evolution.
Are you simply existing?
Confused and clouded with
thoughts about exaltation?
Dream.
Chase something new.
Don't lie to yourself.
Challenge what has been
strategically given.
Give the world something new.
Look inside for compensation
and infinite comparisons.
Eventually the unanswered
questions will suffocate your head of daily
false-fed doctrines.
Be wary of your peers,
specifically the ones who agree
with every bit of force-fed information.

"Bless the house of the Lord."
Wipe your feet on the
white floors of holy visitation.
"You owe us!"
Don't you?
The minute you step through…
Is that really the process
to salvation?
Doing those sacred actions
didn't help me like I had expected them to.
I was naive for many abrupt,
hard years of quick learning.
I had to find my own truth.
"Be worthy to enter the
temple before your life is over."
"Listen to us! We know you crave heavenly
lectures from the mouths of the holy ranked
ones!"
Craving the words of
simple sanity,
are we?
Look at this beautiful world!
You have the ability
to choose what you do with your time here!
This is your perception of reality!
Western religious regimes
are full of greed and brainwashing.

Money! Money is what makes religion laugh
with faith.
They only pretend to hear you.
The cries become deafening.
We are powerful beings!
We are here to break
cycles of lost time,
not fall for someone
else's shortcomings.
Let your mind expand
and meditatively linger
into a state of a high
vibrational existence.
Disconnect from the body.
Find the light in your mind.
Don't fall for the money
grab of organized religion's
corporate ways.
Study the ways of the mind to gain
introspection.
Be aware of the people
trying to take your power away!
We are god.
We are existence.
The universe is you.
It is me.
Existence is everything,
and nothing.

Think with clairvoyance.

I have nothing to lie about.
I am healing my soul.
I no longer care whether or not you believe me.

SAY IT!

Blessed be
You say to me
Kneel and pray
You say to me
The temple is a safe place to be
Be a good person
You say to me
You are not good enough
You say to me
Don't lie
You say to me
Just pray
You say to me
Don't get angry
You say to me
Blessed be
Blessed be
Be yourself
You say to me
Who are you
You say to me
When will you have friends
You say to me
Why are you not better
You say to me
You are not normal
You say to me
And when you watch me suffer…
You say nothing

Sometimes You Have To

It's not the same talking to you, like it used to be.
I have no guilt.
I have no more sympathy.
I thought this feeling would change between you and me.
I thought wrong.
Turns out, I had to let you go to be set free.

IN MY HEAD LIVES STATIC

Inside of my head is where the static speaks.
I tell you the same thing again and again and again.
My mouth is constantly trying to get you to believe.
I see me; you see your defeat.
I see a growing human; you see someone less sweet.
I see someone who needs to face their heart.
You're looking for a cheat.
Facing the problems head-on is the only way to find peace.
I'll be here crying every time you don't believe my pleading verbal piece.
I am not a liar.
I have support that backs me up completely.
I'll sit here crying one last time.
Because even if you got to know me, I don't think you'd like me anyways...

I never saw it coming...

I wish I got to say goodbye to you...

Things We Talk About Now
Just come this way and say
nothing about what you're thinking.
You have the power and will.
The silence sits lingering.
You follow me up the stairs.
I wonder what you're thinking.
I'm just a little girl
fighting the visibility of shivering.
Shaking, I continue to walk.
Then I stop walking.
The room is small.
I switch on the bathroom light,
I try to talk you into leaving.
Waiting and waiting...
It's like you are stalking.
I am asking you to please leave and you don't.
The more time you spend here is getting more frightening.
You insist on my undressing.
When I ask you to leave, you stay right where you're sitting.
All I can do is stand silently,
all the while feeling your eyes pressure me.
I don't want to undress.
I deserve privacy.
But you don't leave.
You watch my clothes hit the floor lightly.
"You can undress in front of me."
You stare,
and I couldn't believe what I was witnessing.
You tell me to stand and wait there for a minute,
as I stand there you sit,
just staring...
You...
And no one will ever know but me.

Future Sight
Started off as a normal day with
breakfast in the morning.
There was no school.
The day seemed oddly quiet for a Saturday.
The crepes were good,
syrup and butter inlaid.
Nothing was out of the ordinary.
I mopped, then put the kitchen
chairs away accordingly.
I went upstairs to hide;
no one bothered me up there,
almost always.
They left for somewhere.
I was watching the kids while
they were away.
The day moved on,
about an hour and a half rolled by.
They shouldn't be home yet.
They walk up the stairs.
I turn off the T.V..
Their faces are blank with no emotion in their
eyes.
I want to hide.
"We need to talk."
Words I never cared to

hear exactly.
Expecting another lecture,
internally rolling my eyes.
I stood there blankly.
"Your mom died last night."
I responded with a blank stare,
eyes burning.
Information denied.
"What?"
I could barely breathe.
This must be a lie.
All emotions hit quickly.
What about a goodbye?
I felt everything and nothing…
My whole life had just changed.
There wasn't enough time...
I quietly stood there.
Blankly staring into the tan carpet under my toes.
"I need some air."
"I need to breathe."
I choked when more tears came.
Clenching my fists, I was filled with rage!
My eyes were swelling with
tension, about to burst from my brain!
How…
How could you leave me?
Why couldn't you stay?

I called your phone,
receiving back only a message box reply.
Your voicemail stayed for about 2 weeks,
I listened to it every day.
I called you often, to cry and to
hear your voice.
I would silently ask about your day.
I called until the message box was deleted.
Then reality replied.

The Day After

Tangible;
  now gone with the wind.
  Sadness.
That meant I was feeling...
Shit.
    I hear your voice in my head.
The tears fall,
        angrily dripping.
  The screaming inside my head shrills with notes of new unwanted beginnings.
    The screaming and asking for answers becomes a coexistent thrill to my daily beginning.
  I want you back!
    I cannot come to terms with what is real.
I'm pretending...
    I feel everything and nothing all at the same time.
    I can't retain which facts are real.
A dream is where I must be living.
  Denial:
something that stays for a while in sly, disguised clothing.
It's not a question about when I will see you again.
  It's the waiting.
Here one day and gone the next.
    I'll eventually come to terms with this new beginning.

A Few Years After
I wish you were walking through
   that door again.
I'm tired of everyone
   talking about going to heaven.
I'm so fucking tired of listening
   to their answers for my depressive moments.
  Turns out, sometimes it's like
day one all over again.
   Permanent denial and reality
start to settle in.
Thinking about all of the
   times we haven't had,
times that should've been.
   All I can do is wonder
about what could've been.
  I try to not give myself reasons to get lost in
thought all over again.
  I sit alone on these same streets
where you kissed my face,
  a face that's grown since then.
   Your face lingers around in my thoughts,
appearing in my dreams of
   lucid anticipation.
I wonder where we
   would be in these current times.
  I never feel the need to
   take a day for granted.
  Everyday holds new
   mysteries and expectations.

When someone
 you love leaves abruptly,
life takes on new
 meanings and captivations.

Reincarnation

Death is not the end,
it is but the beginning.
Many more lives are
waiting to be lived.
Enjoy this one while you have it.
Our souls exist.
Our souls journey has no ending.
We are part of an existence that cannot be destroyed.
We die.
Then we are reborn.
What are you doing with your time here in the land of the living?
Have you learned from the
mistakes in your past lives?
Was it even this world that you lived in?
Love the family you have now.
In the future
you'll have many more to choose from.
Ruled by undisclosed entities there exists
a place where you choose your next reality.
A place of enchantment and wonder.
Futures are planned;
the universe is a beautiful piece of
working machinery.
We need to take care of each other and
enjoy our time here.
This dreamscape is our reality.
Everyone dies.
Death contributes a break
between the lives we will be living.
Our consciousnesses are learning eternally.

    Coming back again and again.
    Dying and returning.
  Coming back again and again,
    for knowledge.
  One lifetime at a time.
Is your soul ready for another beginning?
  You died today;
welcome back
    to the land of the living.

I AM NOT SOMETHING TO BE FIXED.
I AM ON MY OWN JOURNEY.
LIFE IS COMPLEX.
I AM NOT SOMETHING TO BE FIXED.
EVERY LEARNING PROCESS IS PERFECT.
I AM NOT MEANT TO BE FIXED.
THAT WOULD MEAN I WOULD HAVE TO BE SOMEONE ELSE.
MY ROLE ISN'T MEANT FOR THAT.
I AM MEANT TO BE ME.
I AM NOT A PROJECT.
I WILL BE ME NO MATTER WHAT.
I AM NOT MEANT TO BE FIXED.
THERE IS NO CHANGING MY STORYLINE'S SUBJECT.
I AM A MOMENT TO BE LIVED.
A SOUL WITH ITS OWN PURPOSE.
I AM NOT MEANT TO BE FIXED.
I KNOW THIS.

It's hard for me to accept that
people *want* to be around me, because of you.

_____ Believe In You

It's easy to be taught the truth.
What you're told is true.
What you're told is your truth.
Why did I ever have to question you?
I never did question until I could
grasp onto truths without you.
Wait…
I didn't need you.
I understand that you are you.
I understand that you also
only know your truths.
Why couldn't you let me
decide my attributes?
You never even gave me enough
time to learn my own value.
There was never a question,
until my questions redirected your
virtues.
Your truths became my lies.
A truth that lives on and continues.

Righteous

Always righteous,
something I used to stand for.
      Succulent lies that I ate up,
        but now I abhor.
    All of us grouped, then separated,
  because, as equals, no one measures up.
Waiting for visions in a room.
A room where other's identities are now yours to see
 only with luck.

Face

Clouded face.
Waking up.
Windy overpass of luck.
You and me.
We don't match.
You're from this time.
I'm from the past.
Your control didn't last long.
You knew I grew up fast.
You never hesitated to correct my wrongs.
My wrongs were normal human steps.
You were never there.
Your intentions grew where the devil rests.
He rests in your mind-
in what you think is correct.

Weak

Your mind is weak when
running with your lies.
When reality hits, you suffer
from your grand disguise.
You put on a happy face
when others preside.
The two faces you own,
only some have seen.
Only I have seen the second side.
It's not clean.
Face number two comes
out when we're alone.
Sometimes though, there's
been others you've shown.
Alone in your head is where
happiness should be condoned.
You're weak inside.
I've heard all of your different tones.
Taking your anger out on me,
a face no one else knows.

Hero
Hero.
  Somebody I thought
   you were going to be.
    You cannot seem to think freely.
    Why is MY life YOUR destiny?
     You want to prove that control is, somehow, how you're supposed to love me.
      Incredulous love is not healthy.
      You had me blaming myself for things that exist in life harmoniously.
         You created a shell...
        It broke when I finally left freely.
       You left me sitting crying on that couch, desperately.
        The weak mind that appeared...
        It confused me.
       Sitting there confused by your commonsense disability.
       This time,
        is the last time you will hear from my inner peace and stability.

OVERUSED
Pushing sense into this overused term.
The living of life constantly remains firm.
Beliefs of old
that you use to confirm.
Don't think for yourself,
just conform.
The project of life is
a subject that needs explaining.
You're alive, aren't you?
In a world where humans are servants to complaining.
Are you sure? Are you?
Or should I begin my molding?
Your thoughts are mine in the world of the living.
I'll raise you up like someone that loves you,
then end up disappearing.
I'll be gone when your life becomes consistently hard
and depressing.
Hello, my child.
I'm back.
Rest your head on my hardwired engineering.
I am here to help you in this life.
A life cautiously controlled by a
heavenly catering.
Return to us here
to finish your sculpting.
Survive in the beautiful cycle of repeating and ignoring.
Break free from the bonds of lies constructed by a
truthful, hypocritical being.

Eternal

Persistence is key.
Persistence decays thoughts when faced with envy.
　Persistence ended up locking you out of my life completely.
　　Envy wins,
　with the persistence of agony.
　Agony controls the persistence of lonely.
Cautiously holding on with your continuous envy.
A persistence key,
controlled by a lonely, eternal agony.

HELLO LOVELY

It's lovely to see your face this morning.
How are you?
Tell me how you're doing.
I'm doing good,
saying the same three words I'm tired of using.
Obliged to reply,
I send a picture...
smiling.
I'm done on this road,
It's a life sentence to keep on continuing.
I love you too,
but now it's time to stop pretending.

You's

Joking,
   oblivious to the world of you's.
      That sucker in your mouth
         smacks between your lips
           while your brain melts through
              your nose of virtues.
                Thinking in general doesn't
                   suit your nonexistent IQ.
                Thinking,
              or not,
           about your beautified
             survival attributes.
         Attributes of intellect
     fighting with your
   common sense values.
Make fun now.
I'll watch while the ways
      of the world slowly eat you.
          Stop wasting your time,
           start becoming who
          you want to be
        and live how you want to.

Wonder

I ponder on how we've adapted
to thinking in one direction.
Jogging in place.
Dismissing important doctrine.
Ignoring history has never solved the problem.
The idea of endless time
and space doesn't exist-
an entertaining idea to fathom.
The universe's DNA intertwines
with the DNA of all living specimens.
A complicated interface.
Thriving in a unified chaotic system.
Connect to the universe;
you'll connect by disconnecting.
Infinite.
A word that terrifies me.
The expansion of minds
needs to be praised in this
new time of human creation.
Figuring out who we are
in this life leads to pure wisdom.
No one knows the reason
for existence.
We all, somehow, simply exist
in this space-time continuum.
You exist.
Live in a way that excites your being.

Fall in love with existence.

The minds of others is a dangerous place.